talking cats

talking cats

a celebration of the feline spirit

edited by siân keogh

Published in the United States in 2008
by Tangent Publications
an imprint of
Axis Publishing Limited
8c Accommodation Road
London NW11 8ED
www.axispublishing.co.uk

Creative Director: Siân Keogh
Designer: Simon De Lotz
Production Manager: Jo Ryan

ISBN: 978-1-904707-81-3

9 8 7 6 5 4 3 2 1

Printed and bound in China

about this book

Talking Cats brings together an inspirational selection of humorous phrases and sayings spoken from the cats point of view, combined with evocative and gently amusing photographs that bring out the full comedy and pathos of the feline spirit.

These inspiring examples of wit and wisdom, written by real people and their cats, and based on their true-life experiences, sum up the essence of the feline world and its quirks and foibles.

about the editor

Siân Keogh has worked in publishing for several years, producing a variety of books on a wide range of subjects. From the many thousands of contributions that were sent to her by people from all around the world and all walks of life, she has compiled a collection that best sums up how a cat views the world.

I don't repeat gossip,
so listen carefully.

If you can't make your
mark on the world…

Spray the corners.

You know I will out-stare
you everytime.

Who took my ball of wool?

The more attention
I get…

The more I want.

Curiosity just killed
a couple of hours.

I'm afraid there is
no cure for my curiosity.

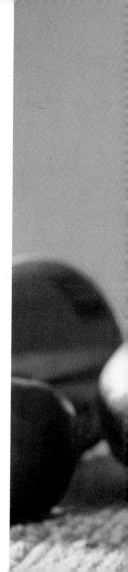

I've overslept and now
I'm late for my nap.

Don't you dare
wake me…

I know where
you sleep.

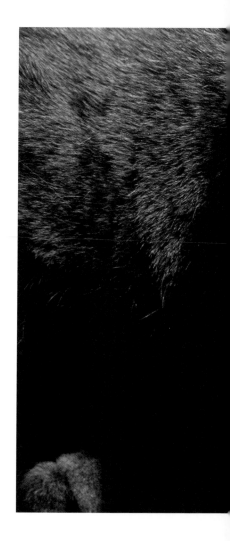

Every time I get the urge to exercise I lie down until it passes.

Every cat has his jungle.

Cats are smarter than dogs. You cannot get eight cats to pull a sled through snow.

Dogs have owners,
cats have staff.

I purr for my own benefit.

You may need to get
me another slave.

Even the stupidest of cats knows more than any dog.

A cat is a hand fed tiger.

A cat will drink his weight in milk,
just to show you he can.

Did I do something wrong?

Sleep fat, walk thin.

When fat, arrange
yourself in slim poses.

Your secrets are safe with me and all my friends.

Milk? What milk?
I didn't see any milk.

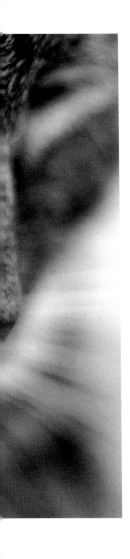

A cat allows you to sleep
on the edge of your bed.

Innocence is the best
form of defence.

Climb your way to the top...

That's why the drapes are there.

A man does not know true rejection, until he has been ignored by his cat.

We can purr our
way out of anything.

Those who do not like cats will come back as mice in their next life.

Tell the truth,
then leave.

If at first you don't succeed, destroy all evidence that you tried.

Every box or basket
should contain a cat.

If winning isn't everything,
why keep score?

If I like it, it's mine.
If I saw it first, it's mine.
If it's in my paws, it's mine.
If it looks like mine,
it's mine.

A basket is the
best place to think.

I hate bad hair days.

I search for food, therefore I am.

A smart cat doesn't let on that he is.

On the internet, nobody knows you're a cat.

I can only please one person per day. Today is not your day. Tomorrow isn't looking good, either.

One cat just leads
to another.

Had I been present at the
creation of the world
I would have proposed
some improvements.

Is that a mouse I see?

Life is tough…

Then you nap.

Never sleep alone,
when you can sleep
on someone's face.

Those who play with cats must expect to get scratched.

A procrastinator's work

is never done.

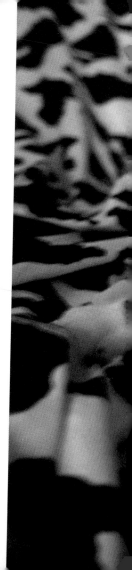

Time spent with us
will never be wasted.

If every dog has his day, then the nights must be all mine.

It's my house really,
they just pay the rent.

If stretching were wealth,
all cats would be rich.

I purr, therefore I am.

Civilization is defined
by the presence of cats.

It's very hard to be polite…

If you are a cat.

All cats look grey
in the dark.

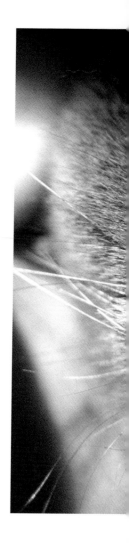

Beware of the people
who dislike cats.

My paws have the
quietest touch.

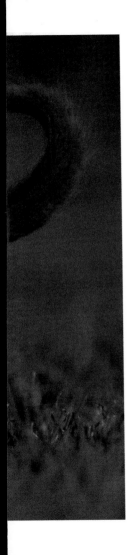

A cat is a lion in a jungle
of small bushes.

No matter what you have done
wrong, always try and make
it look like the dog did it.

My other cat is a Jaguar.